GUIDE TO FINDING LOST
DOGS

ELLA POMPIDOR

www.lostdogtracking.co.uk

Welcome to the
GUIDE TO FINDING LOST DOGS

In the event your dog becomes lost, this book aims to give you the best chance of being reunited with your family member.

Each case will have unique circumstances.

There are many variables that contribute to the likelihood of successfully finding your pet. These include their age, breed, character, health, history, the weather, geography, bystander actions and circumstances around the loss.

The contributing variables are almost infinite.

A trained professional should be consulted, who will consider all the bespoke circumstances and decide what resources are most appropriate.

Not all tactics will work in every case.

Not all options are always available for a variety of reasons.

Above all, try to stay calm and do not give up hope!

RELEASE OF LIABILITY

WE ACCEPT NO LIABILITY FOR THE CONSEQUENCES OF ACTIONS TAKEN FROM THE INFORMATION PROVIDED IN THIS BOOK.

THERE ARE MANY FACTORS THAT CONTRIBUTE TO THE SUCCESS OF LOCATING YOUR MISSING PET.

IN ADDITION TO THIS GUIDE, PROFESSIONAL SUPPORT IS RECOMMENDED SO THAT ALL VARIABLES CAN BE CONSIDERED.

WWW.LOSTDOGTRACKING.CO.UK

CONTENTS

WHAT TO DO IF YOU FIND A LOST DOG	6
ANY DOG CAN BECOME LOST?	7
HOW TO MINIMISE A DOG BECOMING LOST	8
HOW TO INCREASE THE CHANCES OF BEING REUNITED WITH YOUR LOST DOG	10
SCENT SWABBING	11
STOLEN DOGS	13
THE START OF YOUR JOURNEY TO FIND YOUR LOST DOG	14
PROFESSIONAL SUPPORT	15
FINDING LOST DOGS IS EXPENSIVE	16
CANINE SENSE OF SMELL	17
WHAT IS SURVIVAL MODE?	19
WHAT WILL TRIGGER SURVIVAL MODE?	20
HOW LONG DOES SURVIVAL MODE TAKE TO KICK IN?	22
UNDERSTANDING SURVIVAL MODE	23
TYPICAL BEHAVIOURS OBSERVED BY DOGS IN SURVIVAL MODE	24
THE RIGHT AND WRONG WAYS	25
THE DOS	26

THE DO NOTS	28
SEARCH PHASES	30
PHASE 1 – IMMEDIATE SEARCH	31
PHASE 2 – MEDIUM-TERM SEARCH	32
PHASE 3 – LONG-TERM SEARCH	33
LONG-TERM LOST DOGS	34
SYSTEMATIC GROUND SEARCH	36
PROFESSIONALS CONTRACT	39
INFORMATION LOG	40
RELIABILITY SCALE	41
RAISE AWARENESS OF YOUR LOST DOG	44
BENEFITS OF SOCIAL MEDIA	45
DRAWBACKS OF SOCIAL MEDIA	46
MAPPING	47
SPECIALIST LOST DOG TRACKING DOGS	49
POSTER CONSIDERATIONS	51
ANIMAL COMMUNICATORS AND PSYCHICS	53
CAPTURE TACTICS	54
WHAT TO DO IF YOU SEE YOUR LOST DOG	55
REUNION	56
WHAT TO DO IF YOU ARE UNABLE TO CATCH YOUR LOST DOG	57
SUMMARY AND CONTACTS	58

WHAT TO DO IF YOU FIND A LOST DOG

Telephone the owner directly if their details are on the collar or tag.

If the owner cannot be immediately identified, you are required by law to contact the local council (dog warden) and notify them you have found a dog.

You could also:

- Contact local veterinary practices
- Contact local animal shelters
- Notify lost dog/animal social media groups
- Notify local community social media groups
- Notify the RSPCA if the dog is injured or sick

ANY DOG CAN BECOME LOST

- Any breed
- Any age
- Any gender
- All levels of obedience
- Pets and working dogs
- All mobility levels

IT REALLY CAN HAPPEN TO ANYONE!

HOW TO MINIMISE A DOG BECOMING LOST

Some of the circumstances in which dogs become lost are unforeseen and a result of totally random accidents and incidents.

However, **SOME** circumstances are completely avoidable by responsible care management and sensible considerations of environmental factors. Plus, ensuring you have basic training, a good bond and relationship with your dog.

For example:

- Do not allow your dog off-leash in an insecure environment if you do not have a reliable recall.

- Have a correctly fitted harness and collar that your pet cannot back or wriggle out of under stress.

- If your dog has a fear, for example, of thunder or fireworks, do not walk or allow them to be loose in a garden at risky times.

- Ensure garden fences and gates are fit for purpose and secure.

- Do not transfer unknown dogs between areas without two secure points of contact on the lead/harness.

- Do not take risks with **transferring** known dogs in public areas without **a secure lead/harness.**

- Do use positive force-free training to improve your pet's obedience.

HOW TO INCREASE THE CHANCES OF BEING REUNITED WITH YOUR LOST DOG

Ensure your dog has:

- **Up to date microchip details**
- **Been scent swabbed**
- **Valid insurance**
- **Collar and accurate identification tag**
- **Recent photographs**
- **Photographs of identifiable features (scars/markings/tattoos etc)**

SCENT SWABBING

Scent swabbing is the process of capturing the unique smell of each individual dog. If you need advice or assistance regarding this, please contact Lost Dog Tracking (**www.lostdogtracking.co.uk**) We will be happy to assist you.

Use a clean new cloth and rub your pet all over their body, let them play with and bite the cloth and make sure you are happy your dog's unique smell is covering the whole cloth. It is important you do not bath your dog before obtaining the scent swabs, or the cloth sample will smell more of dog shampoo than your pet!

Seal the scent swabbed cloth in a clean container, label with the pet's name and the date the scent swab was taken and place in the refrigerator.

Repeat this process for each dog in your household, ensuring that there is no cross contamination of different pets on individual cloths.

In the event your dog becomes lost, an uncontaminated complete scent picture of your pet is available to our specifically trained tracking dogs.

The scent will need renewing every time there is a significant change in your pet's circumstances, such as long-term medication or neutering, or at 12-month intervals (whichever comes first).

If your dog goes missing but has not been scent swabbed, at the first available opportunity identify something that will smell of your dog. For example, their bedding or collar. Place the item in a sealed clean container/bag and place in the refrigerator. This will preserve the scent for use with a specialist tracking dog.

STOLEN DOGS

IF YOU SUSPECT YOUR PET HAS BEEN STOLEN, CONTACT THE POLICE:

NON-EMERGENCY
DIAL 101

EMERGENCY
DIAL 999

THE START OF YOUR JOURNEY TO FIND YOUR LOST DOG

No two sets of circumstances in which a dog becomes lost will be the same.

There are many and multiple variations that will contribute to how the situation unfolds and changes over time.

The tactics will evolve and change according to varying circumstances.

Your consulting professional should continuously conduct dynamic risk assessments based on the information available at the time.

This booklet is designed to familiarise you with factors to consider should your pet or the pet of someone you know becomes lost. It will give you the best chance of successfully being reunited with your pet in whatever circumstances they went missing.

PROFESSIONAL SUPPORT

ENSURE ANY PROFESSIONAL RESOURCES USED TO HELP, BE IT PAID OR VOLUNTARY, HOLD RELEVANT EXPERIENCE, QUALIFICATIONS AND PUBLIC LIABILITY INSURANCE.

WHAT RESOURCES ARE AVAILABLE?

- PROFESSIONAL SPECIALIST TRACKING DOGS
- PROFESSIONAL DOG CATCHERS
- PROFESSIONAL DRONE PILOTS
- LICENCED REMOTE TRANQUILISER PROFESSIONALS
- ANIMAL COMMUNICATORS/PSYCHICS

FINDING LOST DOGS IS EXPENSIVE

The reality is that the journey of finding your lost dog can be incredibly expensive and time-consuming. Having insurance will relieve some of the financial strain as you may need to pay for the following:

- Professional Resources
- Fuel and mileage
- Stationery
- Posters/advertising
- Food station equipment and food
- BBQ equipment and food
- Telephone/messaging
- Wildlife cameras/trapping equipment
- Binoculars/surveillance equipment

CANINE SENSE OF SMELL

Dogs live in a very different world to humans. Their world is interpreted and navigated by **SMELLS**.

The average dog possesses up to 30 million olfactory (scent) receptors in its nose, compared to about 6 million in a person.

The part of a dog's brain that is devoted to analysing scent is about 40 times larger than that in a human.

In fact, a dog's sense of smell is so great it has been estimated that under perfect weather conditions, they smell a specific scent or object up to 20km away.

Whilst we do not explore the science and anatomy of the canine sense of smell any further here, accepting this ability is critical throughout the journey to recover your lost dog.

The dog's ability to interpret scent is key for both the lost dog's chance of survival and the partnership between the handler and canine of a specialist tracking team.

Whilst humans cannot comprehend the information a dog can ascertain from scents, accepting and trusting the dog's olfaction ability should reassure you that your lost dog is capable (whatever the breed) of making good dog decisions to support its survival.

A dog that has been trained in scent work is directing its natural ability. **ALL** dogs will engage their noses and will naturally do what dogs do best to survive: **SNIFF**.

WHAT IS SURVIVAL MODE?

You will hear the term 'survival mode' a lot once your dog has become lost.

In simple terms, it is where your domesticated pet dog changes its behaviour from the dependent pet you know that has a cooperative relationship with humans to where the dog relies on itself.

It can be emotionally painful for owners to accept their dog is in this mode.

You should not interpret that your dog doesn't love you and doesn't want to come home. It is not that all; he/she is doing what he/she is, as a species, genetically hard-wired to do. **SURVIVE**.

WHAT WILL TRIGGER SURVIVAL MODE?

The individual factors that actually cause a dog to change from a wandering, lost dog to a dog in survival mode and adopting complete feral behaviour are multi-factored. They can include, but are not exclusive to the following variables:

Dog breed

Dog personality

Dog intelligence

Dog history

Dog behaviour

Dog health

Dog navigation skills

Dog reproductive readiness

Circumstances of loss (traumatic or not?)

Owner response behaviour (panic and mania?)

Rescuer behaviour (panic, mania, threatening?)

Weather

Daylight v nightfall

Terrain (urban v rural)

Is the area familiar to the dog?

Bond/relationship with caregiver/handler

Distance of loss location from home

HOW LONG DOES SURVIVAL MODE TAKE TO KICK IN?

It is almost impossible to give a definitive answer. It can be anything from a few minutes, hours, days or more.

However, the more traumatic the circumstances are around the loss, the quicker the dog will transition from domestic pet to survival mode street dog, then into full feral.

If you assume that your dog **IS** in survival mode and act accordingly, you are unlikely to negatively affect the chances of successfully being reunited with your pet.

If you assume that your dog is **NOT** in survival mode, you may seriously inhibit the chance of a successful reunion.

When in survival mode, the owner/capture team must learn to understand, respect and act appropriately in line with the dog's communication and behavioural response in a loss situation.

UNDERSTANDING SURVIVAL MODE

"The very thing that makes your pet dog able to survive when lost is the very thing that makes him difficult to catch."

"The animal is temporarily no longer the pet you know. He must be viewed as having the capability of a wild dog."

"A lost dog will make good dog decisions in order to survive."

"Understanding survival mode is critical to finding a lost dog."

TYPICAL BEHAVIOURS OBSERVED BY DOGS IN SURVIVAL MODE

- Responding aggressively to humans (barking/growling)
- Being secretive, wary, and elusive
- Resting up to 18 hours a day
- Moving locations at dawn and/or dusk
- Establishing regular routes/territory
- Seeking water and food
- Seeking warmth, shelter, and safety

THE RIGHT AND WRONG WAYS

As soon as it is publicly known your pet is missing, you will be bombarded with suggestions from multiple sources about what you should and should not do to locate your lost dog.

The majority of people have good intentions. However, some advice can be seriously detrimental to the chance of a successful reunion.

Relying on the advice of trained regulated and insured professionals is essential.

Here are a few of the absolute **DOS** and absolute **DO NOTS**.

DO............

- STAY CALM.

- IMMEDIATELY AFTER THE LOSS, IF POSSIBLE, REMAIN AT THE LAST PLACE YOU WERE WITH YOUR DOG (THIS WILL ENCOURAGE THE DOG TO RETURN TO YOU).

- DEPLOY PROFESSIONAL RESOURCES.

- UPDATE MICROCHIP STATUS.

- CHECK LOCAL SHELTERS.

- INFORM LOCAL VETERINARY PRACTICES.

- BE PATIENT (AT ALL STAGES OF THE REUNITING PLAN).

- STAY POSITIVE AND FOCUSED.

- ENSURE ACCURATE RECORDS OF SIGHTINGS/INFORMATION ARE KEPT.

- ENSURE INFORMATION IS SHARED BETWEEN THE OWNER AND DEPLOYED PROFESSIONALS.

- ENSURE YOU ARE HAPPY WITH THE COMPETENCY OF PROFESSIONALS AND VOLUNTEERS.

- ENSURE YOU HAVE FRIENDS/FAMILY OR OTHER SUPPORT NETWORKS. IT WILL BE AN EMOTIONAL JOURNEY.

- EMPLOY AS MANY CHANNELS AS POSSIBLE TO SHARE INFORMATION ABOUT YOUR LOST PET.

- RESTOCK FOOD STATIONS DAILY (SAME PLACE, SAME TIME).

- PROVIDE A WATER SOURCE.

- REGULARLY EVALUATE THE EFFECTIVENESS OF TACTICS. WHAT WORKS FOR ONE DOG MAY NOT IN ALL CASES.

DO NOT.........

- Allow anyone who is **STRESSED** and **UPSET** (including the owner) into an area where the lost dog may be hiding. (Cortisol and adrenaline may push a scared pet further away and/or keep them hidden.)

- Organise a ground search party (unless certain conditions discussed later apply) as you are effectively hunting and chasing a lost, scared animal. It is likely to make survival mode kick in sooner and keep the lost dog moving further away).

- Offer a reward (it may encourage people – those with both good and bad intent – to try and "find" your pet themselves using poor techniques).

- Place scented articles of the owner in a food trap or priority areas if the clothing has been worn while they were stressed and upset. ONLY use scented items of owners/home from a happy, stress-free environment.

- Place a urine trail (you are marking territory, and it may keep the lost dog away).

- Give up. No sightings do not mean your dog has died or is not in the area. Its nose will be fully activated in survival mode, and it can smell a further distance than both your eye or a camera can see.

SEARCH PHASES

PHASE 1

IMMEDIATE SEARCH

(First few hours after initial loss)

PHASE 2

MEDIUM-TERM SEARCH

(Days and weeks after initial loss)

PHASE 3

LONG-TERM SEARCH

(Months and years after initial loss)

PHASE 1
IMMEDIATE SEARCH

Maintain static (or long-distance) visual observations

Maintain static position at last known place of dog

Inform microchip company

Contact local veterinary practices

Contact dog warden

Contact rescue centres

Get friends' support

Mobilise professional resources

PHASE 2
MEDIUM-TERM SEARCH

Nominate a team leader

Establish a chain of command for decision-making

Establish information sharing meeting timescales, format, frequency and required persons (Could be a daily information share with team leader and then group professionals once a week)

Establish roles and responsibilities of team members

Set tasks and priorities

Review historical information (once a month is suggested)

PHASE 3
LONG-TERM SEARCH

Monthly professionals information sharing meeting

Monthly resource planning

Monthly review of historical information to ensure nothing has been missed

---

Revisit areas of interest. Remind people your pet is still missing

---

Reinvent posters/leaflets so that people do not become stale. New style and design promotes new interest

A LONG-TERM LOST DOG COULD ……….

- Be surviving well in an elusive feral state

- Have travelled a significant distance outside the local awareness zone, so sightings are not getting reported back to the team

- Have been taken in by someone and not reported as found

- Have been found, but the microchip is not working/not present

- Not be recognised as a lost dog due to a lack of awareness

IF YOUR PET IS LONG-TERM LOST, DO NOT GIVE UP!

THERE IS A CHANCE THAT YOUR PET HAS SADLY DECEASED.

HOWEVER, THERE ARE FAR MORE CONCEIVABLE SCENARIOS WHERE YOUR PET IS ALIVE, WELL AND WAITING TO BE FOUND.

THE REALITY IS A REUNION CAN BE IN A FEW HOURS, DAYS, WEEKS, MONTHS OR EVEN YEARS LATER.

SYSTEMATIC GROUND SEARCH

In the absence of a specialist tracking dog or in an environment unsafe for a tracking dog, it may be necessary to search a specific area with a human team.

For example, if the lost dog is known to be injured or in a critical state, such as after a fight or having been hit by a car.

Ground searching should **NOT** be used if the dog is believed to be alive and well, as it risks pushing the lost dog further away. A lost dog is faster, smaller, and more able to hide than a person.

SYSTEMATIC GROUND SEARCH

- Consult a professional about appropriate use and deployment of tactic.

- **DO NOT** call out to the dog.

- **REMAIN SILENT**.

- **LISTEN** for sounds of distress and movement.

- Move **SLOWLY**.

- Stay **CALM**.

- Check the area thoroughly but slowly, causing as minimal a disturbance as possible.

- Have a canine first aid kit available.

- Search using a logical grid system, ensuring no area is missed.

- Start your search at the last known sighting (the loss point) and expand outwards.

SLOWLY and QUIETLY move forward in one direction as a line

PROFESSIONALS CONTRACT

As the owner, having found your team of professionals, consider generating a contract that stipulates the roles and expertise of each person.

Identify the communication channels and information you expect and require from your team and ensure that all volunteers hold public liability insurance.

If they do not hold public liability, consider a clause that acknowledges personal responsibility for decisions/actions made outside of the agreed plan.

Communicating what is expected and liability held from persons early in an arrangement may prevent any unnecessary upset, confusion or anxiety as the journey unfolds.

A contract will also help filter out those with ulterior intentions and any ambiguity about what responsibilities and accountability people hold.

INFORMATION LOG

Record all information that is given in chronological order on a rolling log.

The log may simply be a handwritten notebook or an electronic rolling document.

An example template is given to demonstrate what information you need to be recording and the type of information to be ascertained from witnesses.

It may be an idea to rate the information that is provided according to perceived reliability. This will help focus resources and direct them appropriately. However, all information must be constantly revaluated for relevance, and as the journey unfolds, patterns form, and circumstances change.

All information MUST be recorded, no matter how trivial it may seem at the time. As the picture unfolds and pieces of information come together and are reviewed over time, one tiny piece of information that may have been deemed irrelevant could become the missing piece of the jigsaw.

RELIABILITY SCALE

LOW	MEDIUM	HIGH
Information lacks detail		Detailed information
Long time delay to report		Reported immediately
Not probable location		Highly probable location
Witness unreliable		Reliable witness
No corroboration		Corroboration
No physical evidence		Physical evidence

This is not an exhaustive list, but it provides an example of how to grade information and direct resources.

RELIABILITY	NUMBER AS PLOTTED ON MAP	DATE	TIME
High	1	01/10/2021	0900
Low	2	02/10/2021	1535
	3		

POSTAL ADDRESS	INFORMANT DETAILS	INFORMATION	OTHER INFORMATION
POCKET PARK ADJACENT TO SMITH LANE AA11 2ZY	MRS CHARLENE PORTER T01234 567 890	WHITE TERRIER WITH BROWN EARS SEEN BARKING AT DOG WALKERS IN POCKET PARK. SIGHTING AT 10 METRES. DOG SCARED AND RAN TOWARDS PARKER LANE	SIGHTING ONE HOUR AFTER LOSS, LESS THAN HALF A MILE FROM LOST LOCATION. INFORMANT WORKS NIGHT SHIFTS FROM 2100. UNABLE TO ANSWER PHONE AFTER THAT TIME
A1234 JUNCTION WITH B5678	MR PAUL SMITHELY T12345 678 901	SMALL WHITE ANIMAL SEEN RUNNING AT SPEED ACROSS A1234. DISTANCE OF 80 FEET. SPLIT-SECOND SIGHTING. INFORMANT WAS DRIVING	THE A1234 IS 60 MILES FROM LOSS LOCATION

RAISE AWARENESS OF YOUR LOST DOG THROUGH:

- SOCIAL MEDIA
- NEWSPAPERS
- MAGAZINES
- POSTERS IN SHOPS
- POSTERS ON BINS
- POSTERS ON LAMPPOSTS
- POSTERS IN RESCUE CENTRES
- COMMUNITY BILLBOARDS
- POSTERS IN VEHICLES
- ROAD BANNERS
- RADIO
- TELEVISION
- RAISE AWARENESS TO MAIL AND DELIVERY PEOPLE, TAXI DRIVERS OR OTHER PROFESSIONS WHO SEE A LOT OF THE AREA DAILY

BENEFITS OF SOCIAL MEDIA

- Reaches a large audience quickly

- Mobilises a large pool of volunteer helpers

- Can provide friendship and support

- Can provide access to professional resources quickly

- Very cost-effective way of sharing information

- Gives access to lost dog groups and appropriate local communities

DRAWBACKS OF SOCIAL MEDIA

- Trolls will post nastiness

- Unhelpful, unqualified "advice" will be given

- Useful information can get lost on threads or go into spam folders

- Can be time-consuming to regulate

- Can be emotionally overwhelming

- Sighting locations can get posted onto threads and missed

- Posted information can be used by dog thieves and charlatans

- Posted information can cause good intentioned members of the community to take "searching" into their own hands

- Not everyone has social media

MAPPING

CHRONOLOGICAL SIGHTINGS ON MAPS

PRINT AND RETAIN MAPS.
IT WILL HELP ESTABLISH PATTERNS OF
MOVEMENT AND SIGHTING HOT SPOTS.

If your pet is long-term missing, start building a second map of ALL the sightings. Even if the scale of the map ends up being so small that you are unable to read village names and details.

One single map with multiple sightings over time will allow a visual representation of areas of interest or travel direction.

More detailed maps are excellent for seeing details of potential shelter areas, crossing areas and water sources.

Therefore, having **BOTH** types of mapping is recommended.

SPECIALIST LOST DOG TRACKING DOGS

Appropriate deployment of a specialist tracking dog will confirm your pet's presence in an area, its direction of travel, and may even directly locate your pet.

The tracking dog will require ideally a scent sample/scent swab of your dog that has the complete and unique scent picture of your dog.

If your dog has not been swabbed, a collar or a blanket belonging to your pet may be sufficient. However, these types of articles are contaminated by a multitude of scents, especially in multi-dog households. They may also not contain the complete scent picture.

The handler will discuss with you all the variables that may affect the success of a tracking deployment.

Factors they will consider include but are not exhaustive to:

- The surface of where the dog was lost (grass, mud, roads, sand etc.)

- The air temperature
- The wind conditions
- The amount of rain/lying water
- The time passed since the dog has been lost
- The accuracy of the information on where the dog was lost from
- Environmental hazards (major roads, rail lines, dense woodland, or non-penetrative foliage)

POSTER CONSIDERATIONS

BOLD, CLEAR LETTERING

COLOURFUL

INCLUDE UP TO DATE PHOTOGRAPHS

CONCISE INFORMATION

INCLUDE ALL CONTACT DETAILS

LAMINATED FOR ADVERSE WEATHER

INCLUDE BASIC DO AND DO NOTS FOR SURVIVAL MODE

LOST DOG—01/10/2021 1800h

Escaped from garden. Male. Microchipped. Neutered. Diabetic (requires medication)

Was wearing blue collar with tag

IF SEEN, TAKE A PICTURE. DO NOT APPROACH OR TRY TO CATCH. NOTE BEHAVIOUR, PRECISE LOCATION & TIME.

CALL or TEXT IMMEDIATELY 24/7

T: 01234 567 890   **M: 07777 777 777**

I AM IN SURVIVAL MODE

I AM FRIGHTENED

DON'T CALL ME

DON'T CHASE ME

DON'T TRY TO GRAB ME

JUST TELL MY MUM WHERE YOU SAW ME, WHAT I WAS DOING AND HOW I LOOKED

ANIMAL COMMUNICATORS AND PSYCHICS

There are many genuine professionals who have achieved amazing results and have many success stories. However, ensure to:

- Verify credibility
- Be careful of scams

Depending on your beliefs, it may or may not be something you wish to consider.

CAPTURE TACTICS

One to One capture, where the lost dog over time approaches the owner, is not always successful.

It may also not be appropriate to use this technique due to location, weather conditions, an unsafe environment, owner unable to be present, or some other variable.

Other capture options can include:

- SCENT LURES TO MORE SUITABLE CAPTURE LOCATION
- TRAPS
- REMOTE TRANQUILISATION

Professional support is needed for all of these tactics.

WHAT TO DO IF YOU SEE YOUR LOST DOG

- ADOPT SUBMISSIVE BEHAVIOUR
- SIT ON THE FLOOR
- STAY STATIONARY IN ONE PLACE
- AVOID DIRECT EYE CONTACT
- REMAIN SILENT IF POSSIBLE
- IF YOU HAVE TO SPEAK, TALK SLOWLY AND SOFTLY
- CAREFULLY PRETEND TO EAT AND ENJOY (NNNMMH NNNHM) FOOD AND GENTLY TOSS TOWARDS THE DOG
- ALL BODY MOVEMENT SHOULD BE CALM AND SLOW
- CONTROL YOUR STRESS LEVELS
- KEEP CALM AND BE PATIENT
- ALLOW THE DOG TO COME TO YOU AND SNIFF YOU
- DO NOT CHASE
- DO NOT GRAB
- DO NOT CALL
- BE PATIENT

REUNION

"As soon as he smelt me, he recognised me and went crazy, tail wagging, happy and so excited."

Once your lost pet recognises you and feels safe, he/she should not bolt if allowed the time to know it's you.

Carefully and slowly apply a harness or collar and lead and secure your pet.

Even if your pet has only been missing for a very short space of time, a veterinary check is recommended.

WHAT TO DO IF YOU ARE UNABLE TO CATCH YOUR LOST DOG:

You must consult a professional to establish which tactic is most appropriate in your circumstances.

There are various tactics that may be used in isolation or combination to support a capture plan:

- Continue One to One capture plan
- Wildlife cameras
- Drones
- Food lures
- Scent lures
- Traps (various varieties)
- Remote tranquilisation (darting)

SUMMARY & CONTACTS

We hope this guide has helped you on your journey to find your lost dog.

If you require further information

OR

If you are interested in training your dog to become part of an accredited and insured specialist lost dog tracking team, please contact:

www.lostdogtracking.co.uk

lostdogtracking@outlook.com

ScentSwabbing@TRACKERDOG.onmicrosoft.com

Copyright © 2021 by Ella Pompidor

All rights reserved. No part of this book may be reproduced or used in any manner without written permission of the copyright owner except for the use of quotations in a book review.

FIRST EDITION

ISBN Paperback (978-1-80227-222-2)
ISBN ebook (978-1-80227-223-9)

www.lostdogtracking.co.uk

Published by PublishingPush.com

www.ingramcontent.com/pod-product-compliance
Lightning Source LLC
Chambersburg PA
CBHW042236090526
44589CB00006B/78